Name : ____________________

Subtraction Worksheets

16	15	10
- 13	- 13	- 8

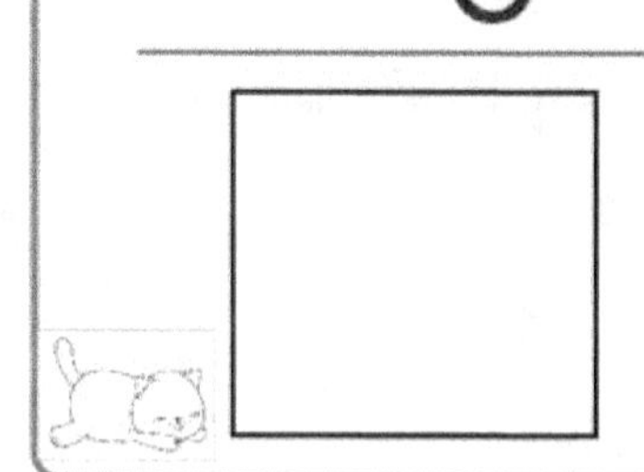

1	9	19
- 1	- 3	- 1

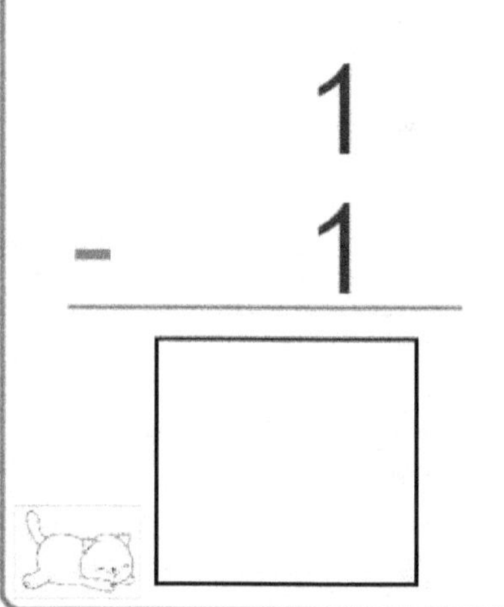

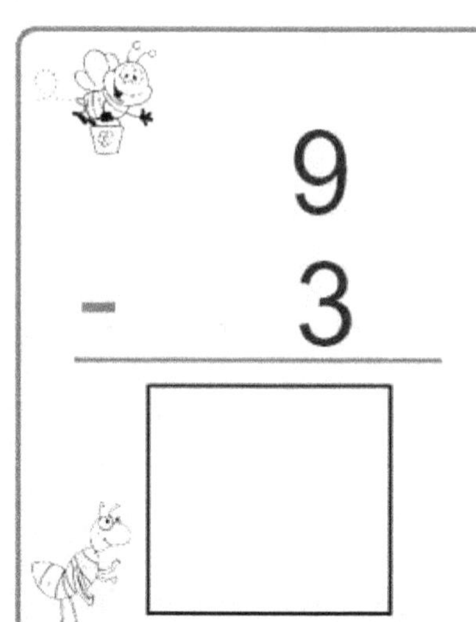

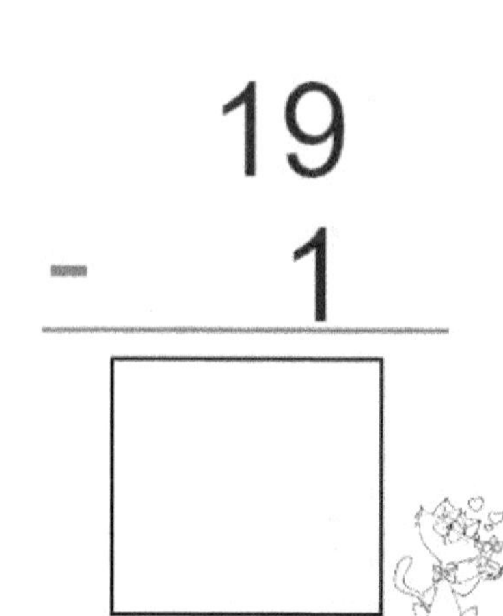

12	9	6
- 4	- 7	- 3

Math Made Easy....

Name : ____________________

Direction: Use the picture to help you find the answer.

1 2 3 4 5 6 7 8 9 10

20 - 12 =	18 - 16 =
19 - 3 =	17 - 2 =
18 - 6 =	13 - 7 =
15 - 1 =	3 - 2 =
15 - 3 =	11 - 5 =

Name : ______________________

Subtraction Worksheets

1 - 1	5 - 3	18 - 5
18 - 2	20 - 3	1 - 1
3 - 1	15 - 6	16 - 11

Name : ______________________

Direction: Use the picture to help you find the answer.

1 2 3 4 5 6 7 8 9 10

19 - 4 =	11 - 7 =
1 - 1 =	14 - 10 =
9 - 2 =	17 - 8 =
19 - 9 =	3 - 2 =
20 - 9 =	15 - 9 =

Name : ______________________

Subtraction Worksheets

17 - 11 ☐	15 - 9 ☐	3 - 2 ☐
7 - 1 ☐	13 - 5 ☐	16 - 6 ☐
9 - 1 ☐	13 - 3 ☐	5 - 3 ☐

Name : ____________________

Direction: Use the picture to help you find the answer.

1 2 3 4 5 6 7 8 9 10

1 - 1 =	4 - 3 =
11 - 4 =	6 - 1 =
4 - 3 =	3 - 1 =
9 - 6 =	18 - 16 =
19 - 13 =	1 - 1 =

Name : ______________________

Subtraction Worksheets

6 − 3 = ☐	18 − 1 = ☐	8 − 4 = ☐
15 − 3 = ☐	3 − 2 = ☐	11 − 1 = ☐
1 − 1 = ☐	6 − 2 = ☐	20 − 11 = ☐

Name : ______________________

Direction: Use the picture to help you find the answer.

1 2 3 4 5 6 7 8 9 10

10 - 8 =	4 - 3 =
12 - 5 =	18 - 4 =
2 - 1 =	3 - 1 =
7 - 2 =	8 - 7 =
15 - 1 =	14 - 8 =

Name : ______________________

Subtraction Worksheets

5 - 3	15 - 6	16 - 14
2 - 1	1 - 1	6 - 4
5 - 3	20 - 5	3 - 2

Math Made Easy....

Name : ______________________________

Direction: Use the picture to help you find the answer.

1 2 3 4 5 6 7 8 9 10

13 - 7 =

18 - 12 =

13 - 11 =

7 - 6 =

4 - 2 =

20 - 2 =

11 - 4 =

15 - 6 =

10 - 7 =

11 - 7 =

Name : ____________________

Subtraction Worksheets

12 − 10 = ☐	19 − 5 = ☐	8 − 4 = ☐
4 − 2 = ☐	3 − 2 = ☐	13 − 3 = ☐
12 − 6 = ☐	4 − 3 = ☐	9 − 3 = ☐

Name : ____________________

Direction: Use the picture to help you find the answer.

1 2 3 4 5 6 7 8 9 10

1 - 1 =

1 - 1 =

1 - 1 =

18 - 7 =

19 - 11 =

5 - 3 =

6 - 4 =

9 - 8 =

6 - 5 =

18 - 8 =

Name : ______________________

Subtraction Worksheets

11 − 8 = ☐	11 − 3 = ☐	13 − 5 = ☐
16 − 13 = ☐	7 − 5 = ☐	8 − 3 = ☐
10 − 1 = ☐	13 − 1 = ☐	3 − 1 = ☐

Name : ____________________

Direction: Use the picture to help you find the answer.

1 2 3 4 5 6 7 8 9 10

15 - 4 =	10 - 6 =
6 - 4 =	17 - 11 =
13 - 4 =	19 - 9 =
7 - 1 =	13 - 8 =
15 - 13 =	6 - 5 =

Name : ____________________

Subtraction Worksheets

20 - 16	19 - 5	12 - 11
2 - 1	1 - 1	5 - 3
3 - 1	17 - 13	16 - 6

Name : ___________________________

Direction: Use the picture to help you find the answer.

1	2	3	4	5	6	7	8	9	10
☆	☆	☆	☆	☆	☆	☆	☆	☆	☆

19 - 13 =

6 - 2 =

3 - 2 =

10 - 6 =

2 - 1 =

15 - 9 =

5 - 1 =

1 - 1 =

1 - 1 =

7 - 2 =

Name : ______________________

Subtraction Worksheets

19 − 11 = ☐	5 − 4 = ☐	2 − 1 = ☐
19 − 13 = ☐	12 − 11 = ☐	14 − 3 = ☐
15 − 8 = ☐	16 − 8 = ☐	6 − 5 = ☐

Name : ________________

Direction: Use the picture to help you find the answer.

1 2 3 4 5 6 7 8 9 10

4 - 3 =	20 - 1 =
19 - 3 =	7 - 4 =
15 - 4 =	19 - 18 =
4 - 1 =	17 - 6 =
20 - 11 =	13 - 10 =

Name : ______________________

Subtraction Worksheets

16 − 14 = ☐	19 − 1 = ☐	2 − 1 = ☐
14 − 4 = ☐	3 − 2 = ☐	20 − 11 = ☐
17 − 2 = ☐	1 − 1 = ☐	9 − 7 = ☐

Name : ________________

Direction: Use the picture to help you find the answer.

1 2 3 4 5 6 7 8 9 10

8 - 4 =	5 - 3 =
1 - 1 =	12 - 4 =
14 - 9 =	5 - 3 =
13 - 8 =	9 - 6 =
16 - 6 =	11 - 6 =

Name : ______________________

Subtraction Worksheets

15 − 14 = ☐	8 − 2 = ☐	1 − 1 = ☐
10 − 6 = ☐	6 − 4 = ☐	18 − 5 = ☐
9 − 2 = ☐	11 − 8 = ☐	1 − 1 = ☐

Name : ______________________

Direction: Use the picture to help you find the answer.

1 2 3 4 5 6 7 8 9 10

16 - 9 =	20 - 15 =
13 - 9 =	1 - 1 =
12 - 11 =	5 - 2 =
19 - 3 =	15 - 14 =
14 - 6 =	14 - 1 =

Name : ____________________

Subtraction Worksheets

7 - 4 ☐	20 - 14 ☐	5 - 3 ☐
5 - 4 ☐	3 - 1 ☐	17 - 16 ☐
12 - 7 ☐	17 - 14 ☐	14 - 9 ☐

Name : ______________________________

Direction: Use the picture to help you find the answer.

1 2 3 4 5 6 7 8 9 10

13 - 6 =	8 - 1 =
4 - 3 =	9 - 5 =
10 - 8 =	1 - 1 =
13 - 3 =	4 - 1 =
13 - 11 =	11 - 6 =

Name : ____________________

Subtraction Worksheets

1 - 1 = ☐	8 - 7 = ☐	4 - 2 = ☐
20 - 15 = ☐	8 - 7 = ☐	6 - 5 = ☐
17 - 10 = ☐	17 - 8 = ☐	14 - 7 = ☐

Name : ______________________

Direction: Use the picture to help you find the answer.

1 2 3 4 5 6 7 8 9 10

18 - 2 =

2 - 1 =

4 - 1 =

16 - 11 =

19 - 9 =

7 - 2 =

15 - 9 =

5 - 3 =

13 - 11 =

11 - 10 =

Name : ____________________

Subtraction Worksheets

16 - 9	18 - 10	5 - 2
18 - 8	7 - 5	16 - 13
17 - 16	10 - 5	16 - 14

Name : ____________________

Direction: Use the picture to help you find the answer.

1 2 3 4 5 6 7 8 9 10

2 - 1 =	2 - 1 =
14 - 10 =	18 - 8 =
1 - 1 =	8 - 7 =
6 - 3 =	20 - 7 =
7 - 2 =	3 - 1 =

Name : ______________________

Subtraction Worksheets

9 − 6 = ☐	7 − 1 = ☐	20 − 6 = ☐
5 − 1 = ☐	5 − 1 = ☐	4 − 1 = ☐
19 − 3 = ☐	10 − 5 = ☐	7 − 5 = ☐

Name : ______________________________

Direction: Use the picture to help you find the answer.

1	2	3	4	5	6	7	8	9	10

12 - 11 =

8 - 7 =

16 - 7 =

12 - 3 =

9 - 6 =

14 - 9 =

1 - 1 =

10 - 5 =

15 - 11 =

6 - 4 =

Name : ______________________

Subtraction Worksheets

18 - 12	14 - 6	1 - 1
3 - 2	5 - 4	11 - 4
6 - 4	3 - 1	15 - 5

Name : ______________________

Direction: Use the picture to help you find the answer.

1 2 3 4 5 6 7 8 9 10

20 - 8 =

5 - 3 =

12 - 2 =

15 - 12 =

17 - 4 =

13 - 5 =

8 - 7 =

17 - 11 =

16 - 11 =

3 - 1 =

Name : ______________________

Subtraction Worksheets

16 − 1 = ☐	12 − 10 = ☐	6 − 2 = ☐
5 − 2 = ☐	18 − 5 = ☐	10 − 9 = ☐
12 − 8 = ☐	3 − 2 = ☐	8 − 6 = ☐

Name : ____________________

Direction: Use the picture to help you find the answer.

1 2 3 4 5 6 7 8 9 10

1 - 1 =	6 - 4 =
4 - 1 =	19 - 12 =
7 - 3 =	14 - 9 =
14 - 11 =	12 - 11 =
11 - 3 =	15 - 14 =

Name : ______________________________

Subtraction Worksheets

5 - 1	10 - 2	15 - 2
12 - 1	5 - 2	11 - 6
17 - 14	18 - 12	3 - 1

Name : ______________________

Direction: Use the picture to help you find the answer.

1 2 3 4 5 6 7 8 9 10

20 - 11 =	5 - 4 =
14 - 7 =	16 - 6 =
3 - 2 =	19 - 8 =
17 - 4 =	9 - 6 =
20 - 1 =	3 - 1 =

Name : ______________________________

Subtraction Worksheets

18 − 9	5 − 1	8 − 4
11 − 4	8 − 7	15 − 7
16 − 14	8 − 1	11 − 1

Name : ______________________________

Direction: Use the picture to help you find the answer.

1 2 3 4 5 6 7 8 9 10

9 - 5 =	12 - 6 =
3 - 1 =	7 - 6 =
1 - 1 =	20 - 8 =
10 - 1 =	13 - 3 =
13 - 9 =	13 - 10 =

Name : ______________________

Subtraction Worksheets

6 - 4 = ☐	13 - 3 = ☐	12 - 11 = ☐
1 - 1 = ☐	1 - 1 = ☐	13 - 5 = ☐
2 - 1 = ☐	6 - 2 = ☐	16 - 7 = ☐

Name : ____________________

Direction: Use the picture to help you find the answer.

1 2 3 4 5 6 7 8 9 10

3 - 1 =	16 - 7 =
13 - 5 =	14 - 5 =
12 - 8 =	16 - 11 =
9 - 2 =	6 - 1 =
8 - 6 =	12 - 5 =

Name : ______________________

Subtraction Worksheets

13 − 6 = ☐	13 − 9 = ☐	20 − 17 = ☐
11 − 2 = ☐	6 − 5 = ☐	18 − 4 = ☐
4 − 2 = ☐	1 − 1 = ☐	20 − 16 = ☐

Math Made Easy....

Name : ____________________

Direction: Use the picture to help you find the answer.

1 2 3 4 5 6 7 8 9 10

17 - 5 =	15 - 8 =
5 - 3 =	1 - 1 =
16 - 12 =	8 - 4 =
5 - 4 =	19 - 10 =
12 - 6 =	9 - 7 =

Name : ______________________

Subtraction Worksheets

11 − 6 = ☐	12 − 8 = ☐	2 − 1 = ☐
15 − 11 = ☐	10 − 8 = ☐	3 − 1 = ☐
18 − 16 = ☐	16 − 1 = ☐	1 − 1 = ☐

Name : ______________________

Direction: Use the picture to help you find the answer.

1 2 3 4 5 6 7 8 9 10

8 - 7 =	16 - 13 =
19 - 8 =	7 - 4 =
20 - 4 =	9 - 2 =
7 - 3 =	6 - 2 =
6 - 3 =	19 - 16 =

Name : ______________________

Subtraction Worksheets

13 − 5 = ☐	8 − 5 = ☐	5 − 2 = ☐
19 − 4 = ☐	19 − 6 = ☐	12 − 11 = ☐
18 − 11 = ☐	7 − 6 = ☐	13 − 11 = ☐

Name : ______________________________

Direction: Use the picture to help you find the answer.

1 2 3 4 5 6 7 8 9 10

5 - 2 =	10 - 3 =
19 - 3 =	5 - 2 =
3 - 2 =	8 - 1 =
3 - 2 =	7 - 3 =
9 - 4 =	11 - 2 =

Name : ______________________

Subtraction Worksheets

2 − 1 = ☐	8 − 1 = ☐	17 − 9 = ☐
16 − 11 = ☐	11 − 10 = ☐	16 − 10 = ☐
9 − 8 = ☐	5 − 4 = ☐	10 − 7 = ☐

Name : ______________________

Direction: Use the picture to help you find the answer.

1 2 3 4 5 6 7 8 9 10

6 - 1 =	13 - 10 =
15 - 3 =	16 - 2 =
10 - 3 =	2 - 1 =
11 - 5 =	7 - 2 =
13 - 3 =	3 - 2 =

Name : ____________________

Subtraction Worksheets

5 - 4	7 - 3	11 - 2
6 - 2	1 - 1	3 - 1
19 - 15	6 - 1	11 - 9

Name : ______________________

Direction: Use the picture to help you find the answer.

1 2 3 4 5 6 7 8 9 10

19 - 2 =

5 - 1 =

4 - 3 =

9 - 8 =

12 - 11 =

20 - 4 =

13 - 1 =

9 - 2 =

8 - 4 =

14 - 5 =

Name :

Subtraction Worksheets

3 - 1	11 - 6	1 - 1
17 - 4	18 - 17	10 - 3
2 - 1	3 - 1	1 - 1

Name : ______________________

Addition Worksheets

20 + 6 = ☐	7 + 7 = ☐	11 + 7 = ☐
16 + 8 = ☐	14 + 18 = ☐	6 + 11 = ☐
14 + 16 = ☐	20 + 5 = ☐	19 + 2 = ☐

Name : ______________________

Addition Worksheets

20 + 6 = ☐	7 + 7 = ☐	11 + 7 = ☐
16 + 8 = ☐	14 + 18 = ☐	6 + 11 = ☐
14 + 16 = ☐	20 + 5 = ☐	19 + 2 = ☐

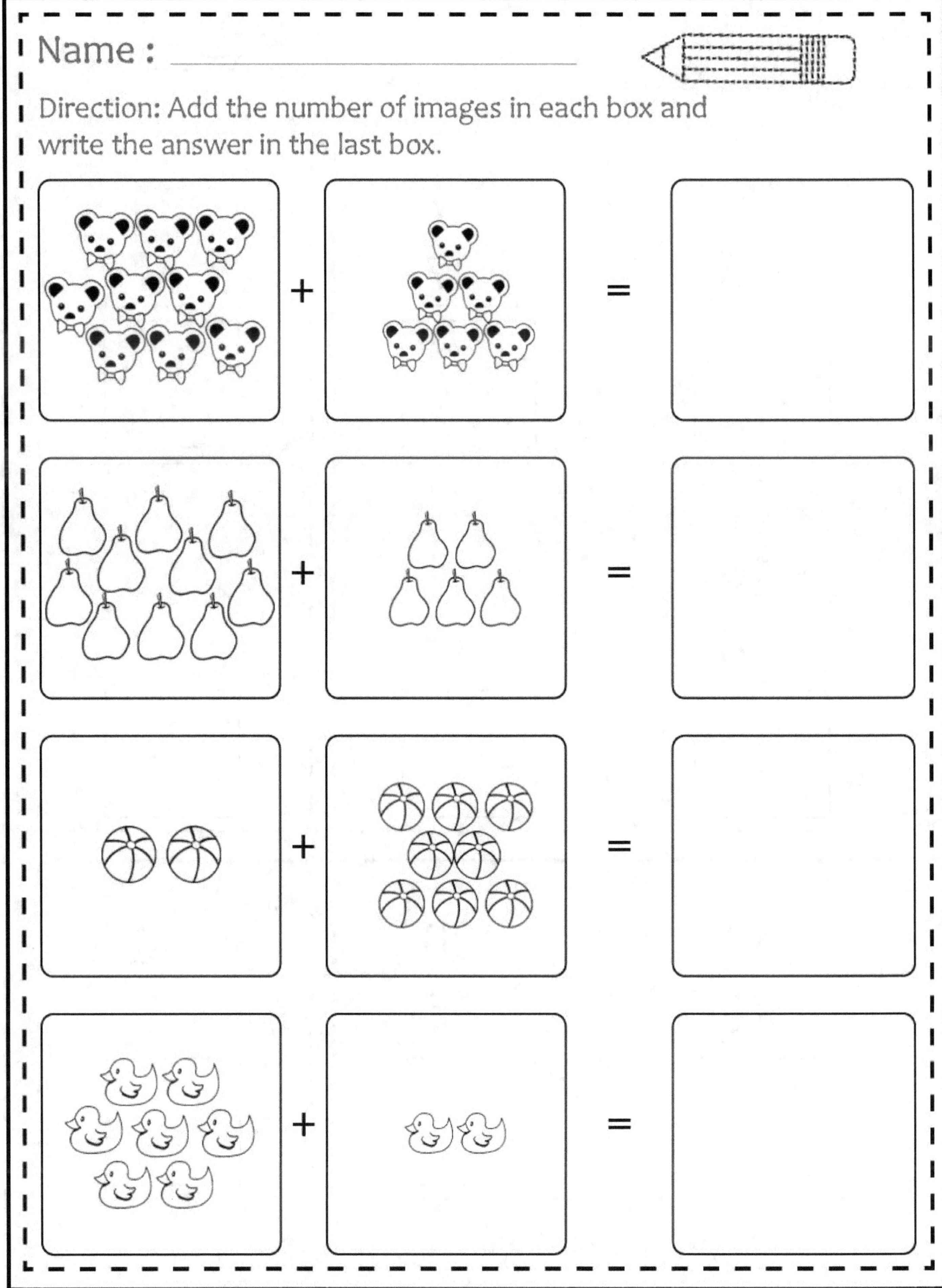
Name :
Direction: Add the number of images in each box and
write the answer in the last box.
+
=
+
=
+
=
+
=

Name : ______________________

Addition Worksheets

4 + 4 = ☐ Answer	1 + 10 = ☐ Answer
5 + 9 = ☐ Answer	2 + 4 = ☐ Answer
1 + 1 = ☐ Answer	2 + 10 = ☐ Answer

Name : ______________________

Addition Worksheets

17 + 18 = ☐	8 + 7 = ☐	15 + 11 = ☐
12 + 19 = ☐	13 + 4 = ☐	5 + 14 = ☐
18 + 19 = ☐	3 + 2 = ☐	5 + 15 = ☐

Name : ____________________

Direction: Add the number of images in each box and write the answer in the last box.

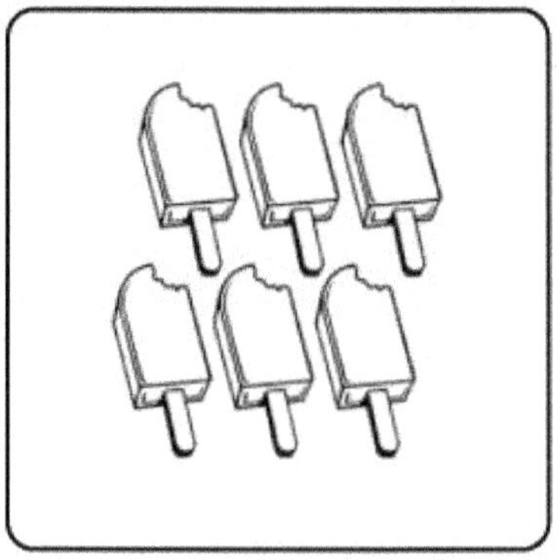

+ 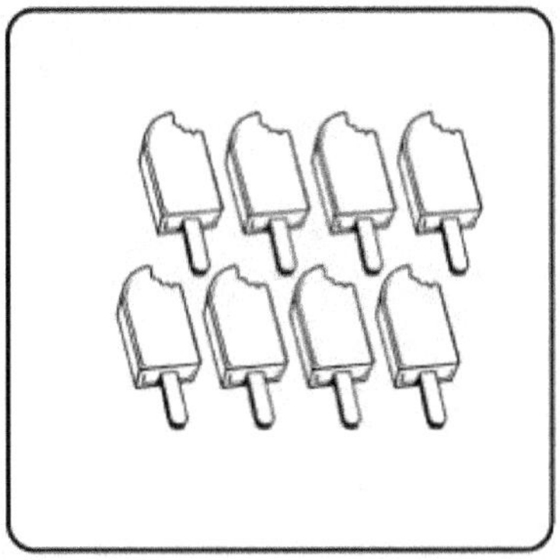 =

+  =

+  =

+ 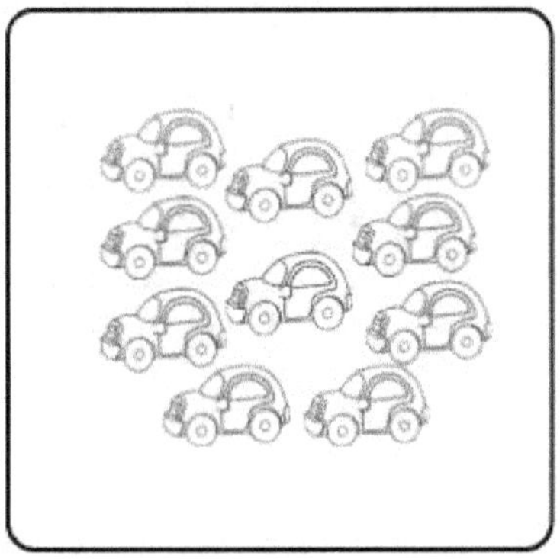 =

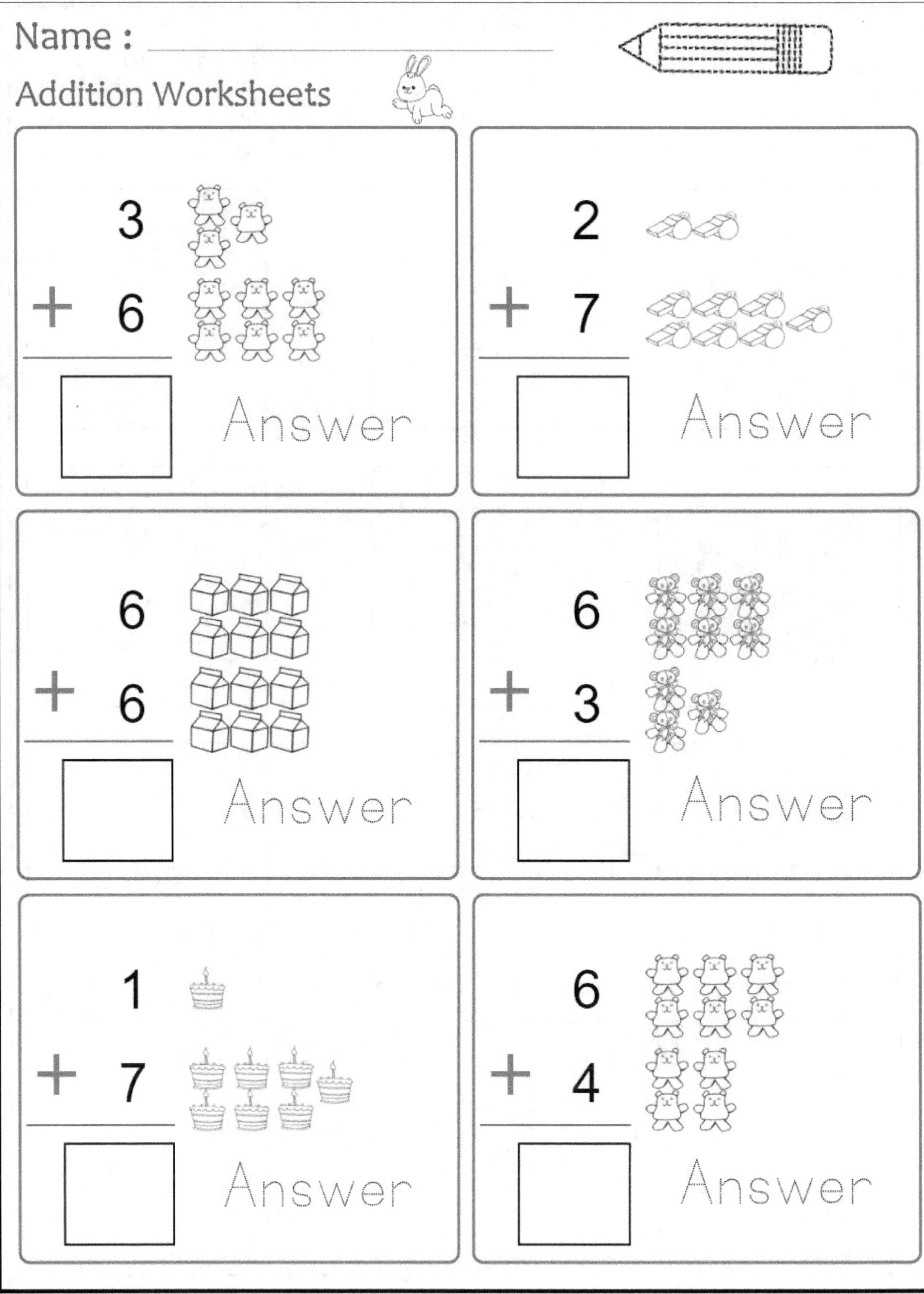

Name :
Addition Worksheets
3
+ 6
Answer
2
+ 7
Answer
6
+ 6
Answer
6
+ 3
Answer
1
+ 7
Answer
6
+ 4
Answer

Name : ______________________

Addition Worksheets

11 + 8 = ☐	6 + 11 = ☐	8 + 3 = ☐
8 + 3 = ☐	15 + 14 = ☐	5 + 15 = ☐
19 + 18 = ☐	12 + 1 = ☐	2 + 19 = ☐

Name : ____________________

Direction: Add the number of images in each box and write the answer in the last box.

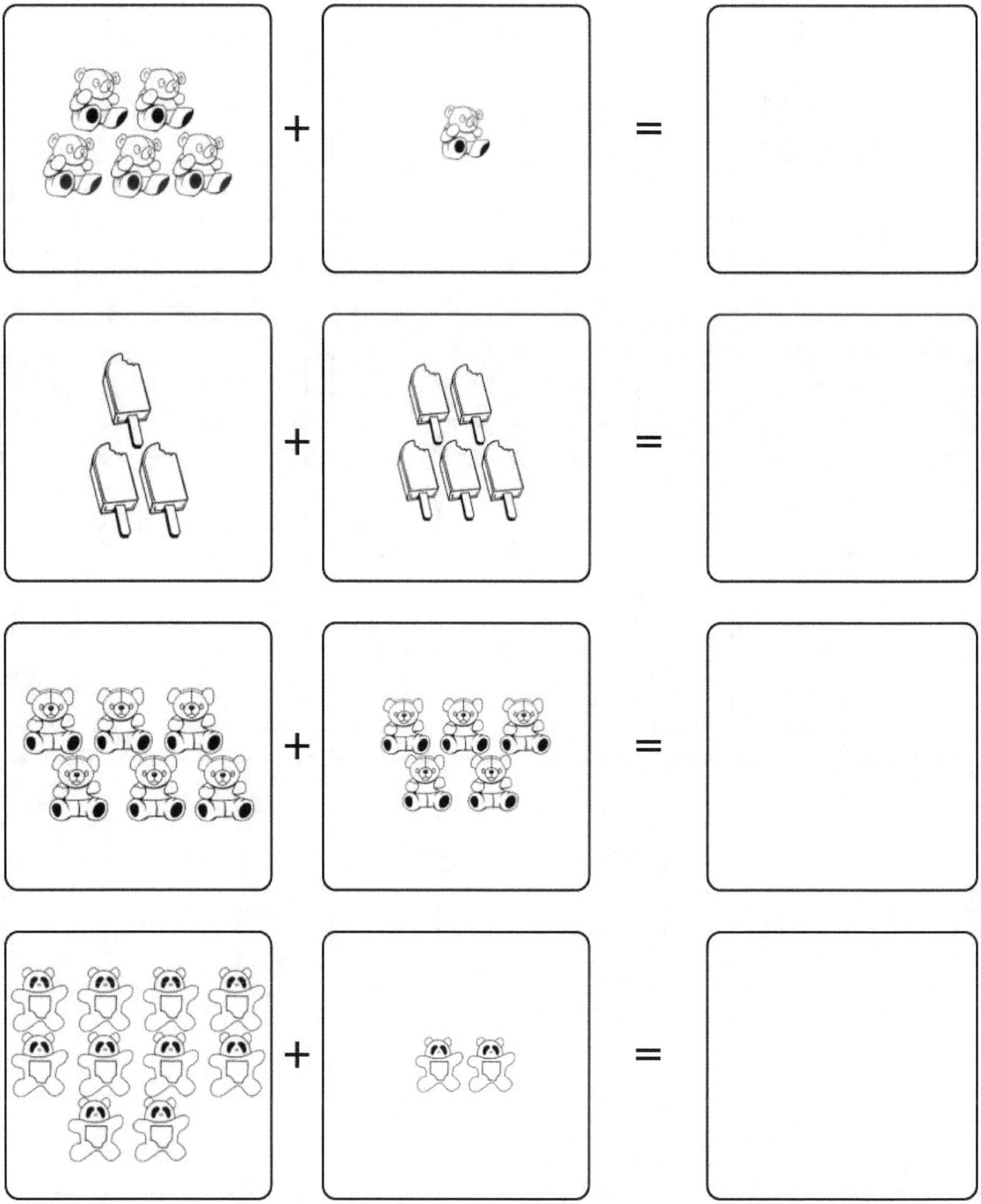

+ =

+ =

+ =

+ =

Name : ______________________

Addition Worksheets

3 + 7 ___ ☐ Answer	2 + 5 ___ ☐ Answer
1 + 9 ___ ☐ Answer	6 + 2 ___ ☐ Answer
5 + 8 ___ ☐ Answer	2 + 6 ___ ☐ Answer

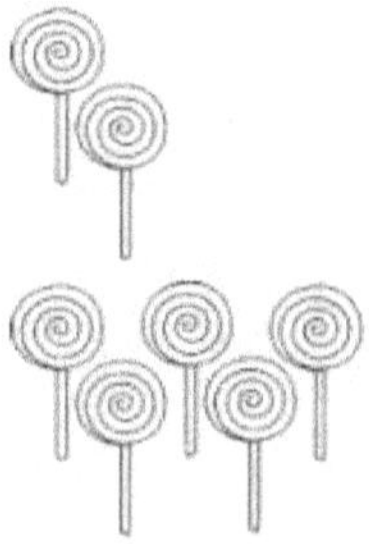

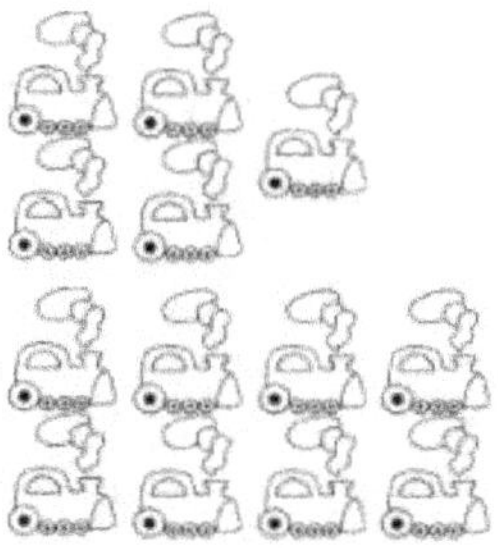

Name : ______________________

Addition Worksheets

8 + 10 = ☐	17 + 1 = ☐	1 + 2 = ☐
7 + 5 = ☐	6 + 10 = ☐	18 + 16 = ☐
5 + 4 = ☐	13 + 7 = ☐	4 + 5 = ☐

Name : ______________________

Direction: Add the number of images in each box and write the answer in the last box.

+  =

+  =

+  =

+  =

Name : ______________________

Addition Worksheets

$$2 + 2 = \square$$

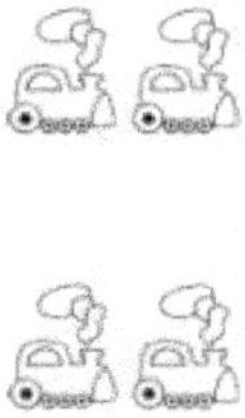

Answer

$$2 + 4 = \square$$

Answer

$$2 + 1 = \square$$

Answer

$$6 + 5 = \square$$

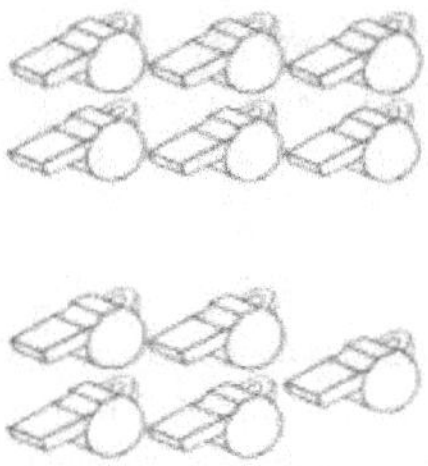

Answer

$$1 + 6 = \square$$

Answer

$$6 + 1 = \square$$

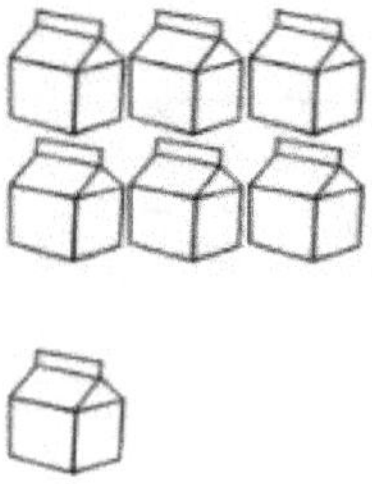

Answer

Name : ______________________

Addition Worksheets

18 + 11 = ☐	16 + 12 = ☐	11 + 4 = ☐
3 + 7 = ☐	14 + 19 = ☐	19 + 14 = ☐
8 + 20 = ☐	9 + 6 = ☐	5 + 18 = ☐

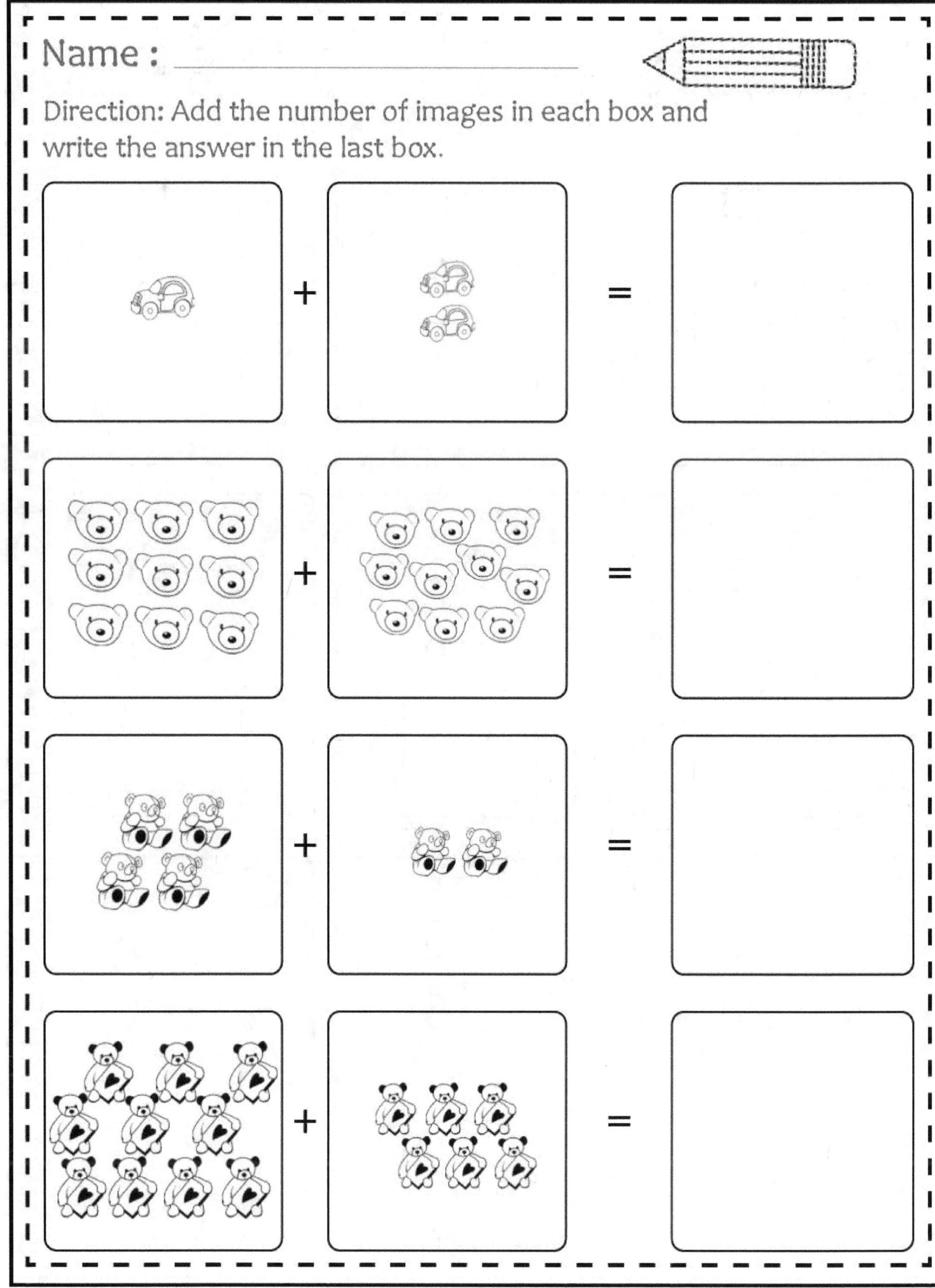
Name : ____________________
Direction: Add the number of images in each box and
write the answer in the last box.
+
=
+
=
+
=
+
=

Name : ____________________

Addition Worksheets

4 + 3 ☐ Answer	5 + 8 ☐ Answer
6 + 1 ☐ Answer	4 + 1 ☐ Answer
3 + 5 ☐ Answer	1 + 9 ☐ Answer

Name :

Addition Worksheets

15	11	2
+ 7	+ 5	+ 7

12	14	6
+ 2	+ 15	+ 18

18	7	18
+ 9	+ 6	+ 4

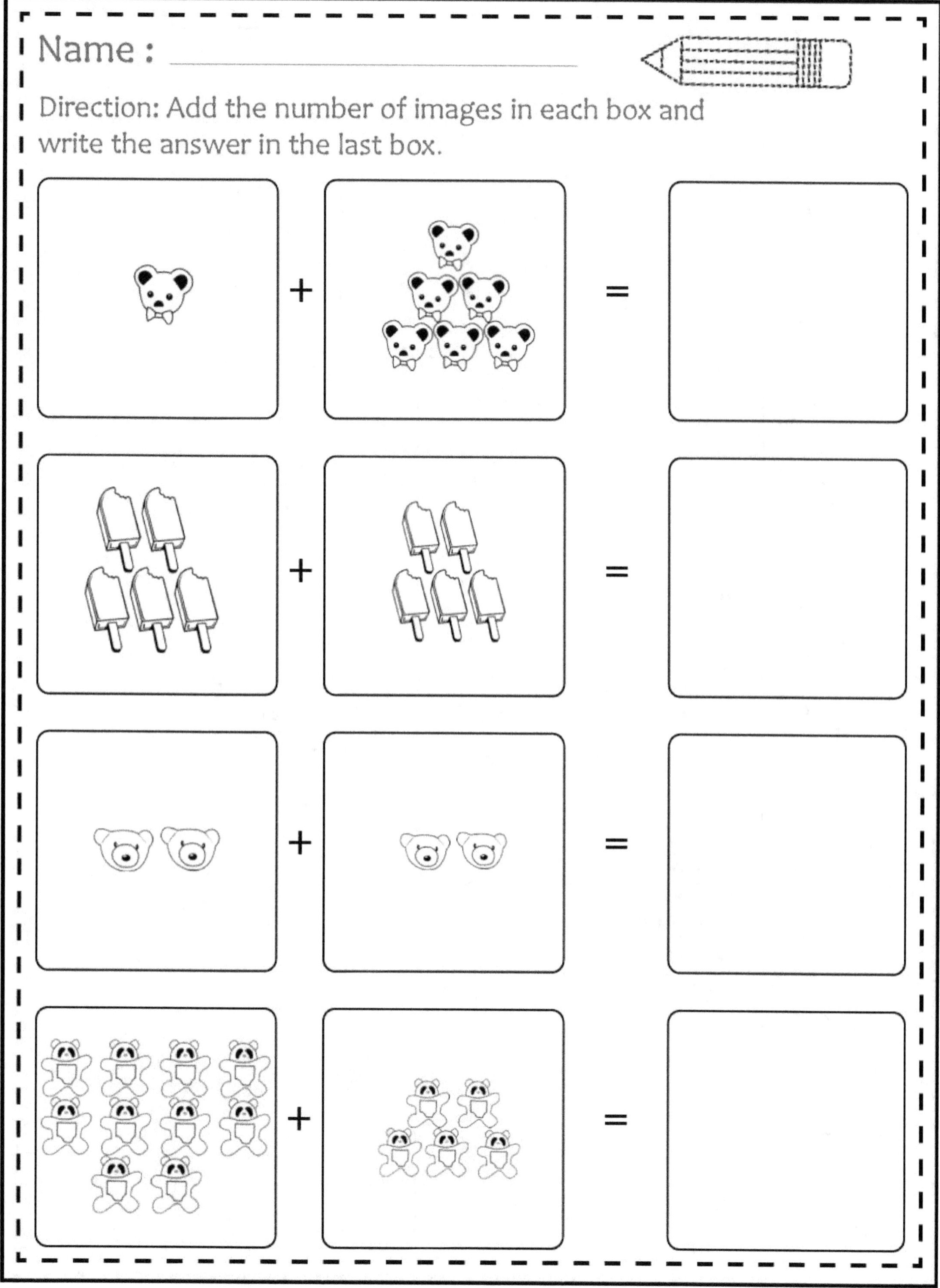
Name :
Direction: Add the number of images in each box and write the answer in the last box.
+
=
+
=
+
=
+
=

Name : ____________________

Addition Worksheets

4 + 6 Answer	3 + 3 Answer
1 + 7 Answer	5 + 8 Answer
5 + 4 Answer	1 + 8 Answer

Name : ______________________

Addition Worksheets

1 + 12 = ☐	14 + 5 = ☐	7 + 4 = ☐
12 + 17 = ☐	13 + 16 = ☐	18 + 9 = ☐
15 + 18 = ☐	1 + 15 = ☐	20 + 10 = ☐

Name : ________________________

Direction: Add the number of images in each box and write the answer in the last box.

+ =

+ =

+ =

+ =

Name : ______________________

Addition Worksheets

2 + 9 ☐ Answer	5 + 7 ☐ Answer
3 + 6 ☐ Answer	6 + 1 ☐ Answer
1 + 6 ☐ Answer	3 + 4 ☐ Answer

Name : ______________________________

Addition Worksheets

20 + 1 = ☐	1 + 12 = ☐	20 + 1 = ☐
12 + 1 = ☐	16 + 18 = ☐	20 + 10 = ☐
5 + 5 = ☐	17 + 20 = ☐	4 + 14 = ☐

Name : ______________________

Direction: Add the number of images in each box and write the answer in the last box.

+  =

+  =

+  =

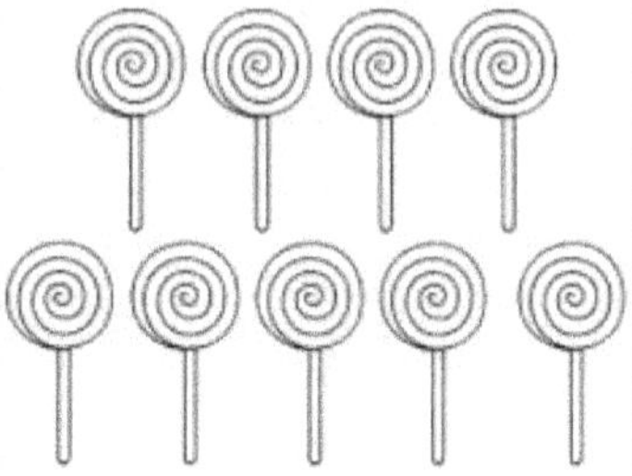

+  =

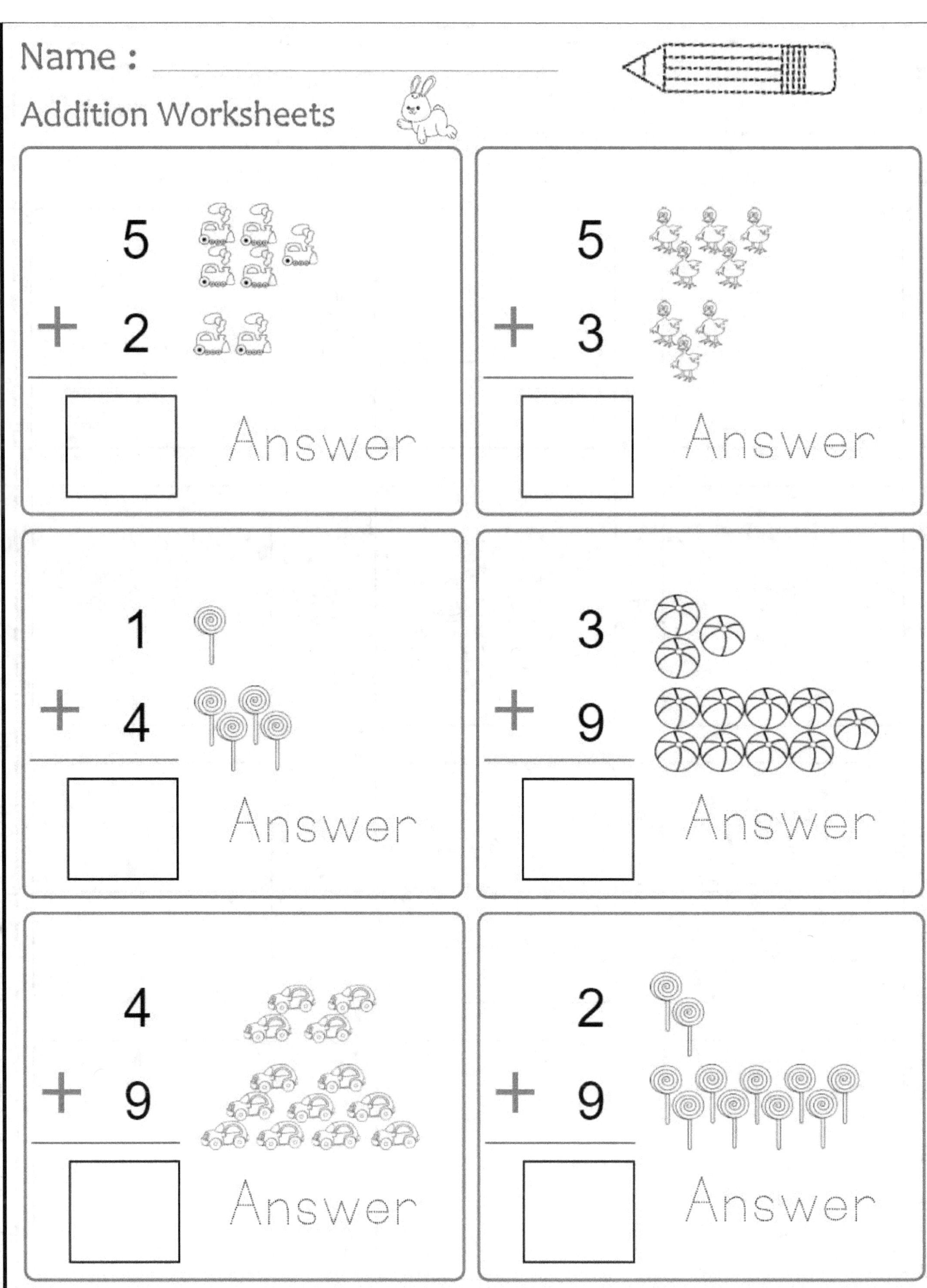

Name : ____________________

Addition Worksheets

5 + 2	Answer	5 + 3	Answer
1 + 4	Answer	3 + 9	Answer
4 + 9	Answer	2 + 9	Answer

Name : ____________________

Addition Worksheets

9 + 12 = ☐	11 + 11 = ☐	5 + 8 = ☐
1 + 17 = ☐	6 + 19 = ☐	17 + 14 = ☐
4 + 13 = ☐	12 + 16 = ☐	8 + 20 = ☐

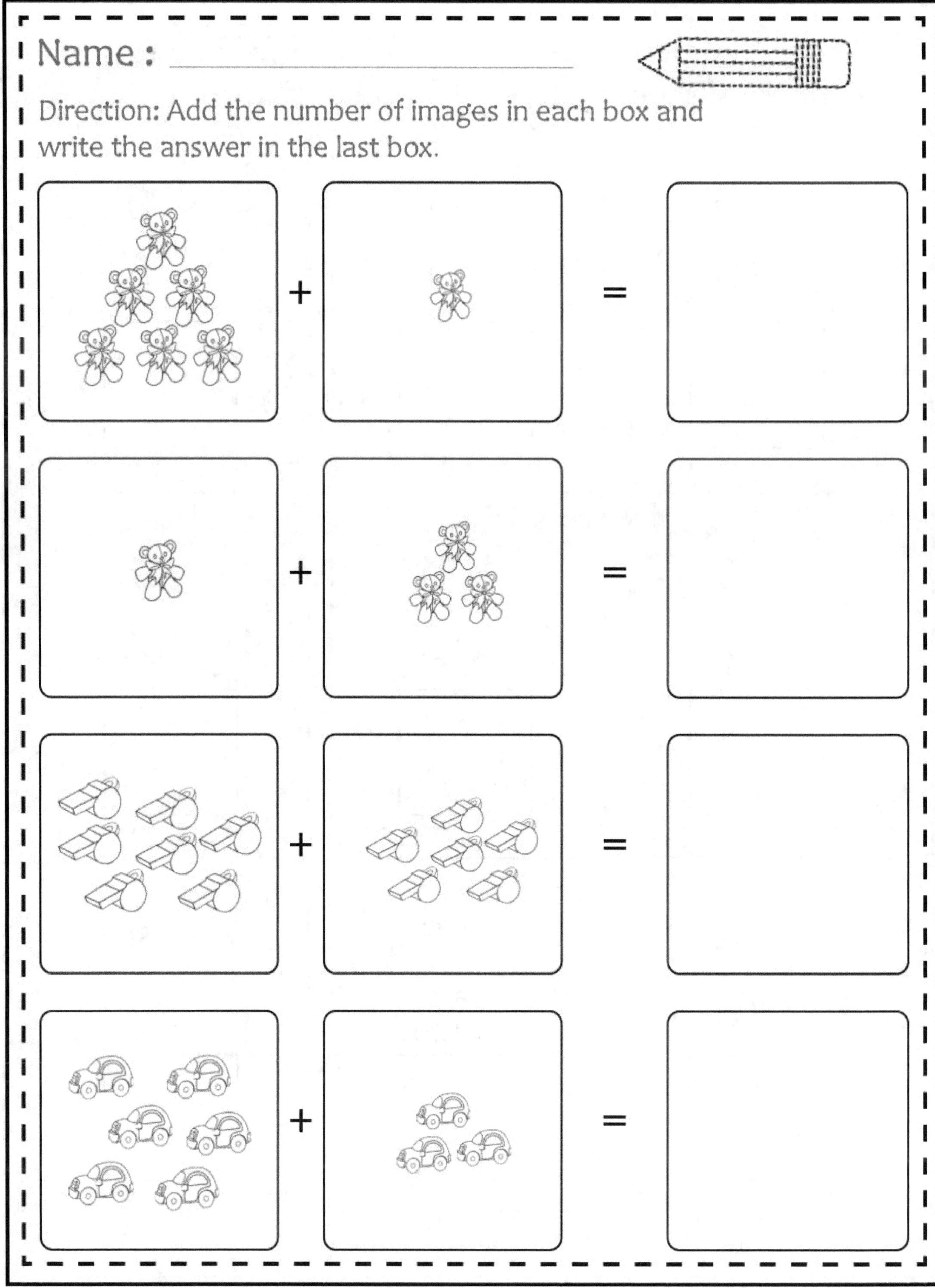

Name :
Direction: Add the number of images in each box and write the answer in the last box.
+
=
+
=
+
=
+
=

Name : ________________________

Addition Worksheets

6 + 7 ___ ☐ Answer	3 + 9 ___ ☐ Answer
5 + 10 ___ ☐ Answer	3 + 4 ___ ☐ Answer
1 + 3 ___ ☐ Answer	6 + 4 ___ ☐ Answer

Name : ______________________________

Addition Worksheets

1 + 12 = ☐	8 + 1 = ☐	3 + 12 = ☐
18 + 20 = ☐	5 + 9 = ☐	17 + 14 = ☐
13 + 9 = ☐	12 + 11 = ☐	11 + 3 = ☐

Name : ______________________

Direction: Add the number of images in each box and write the answer in the last box.

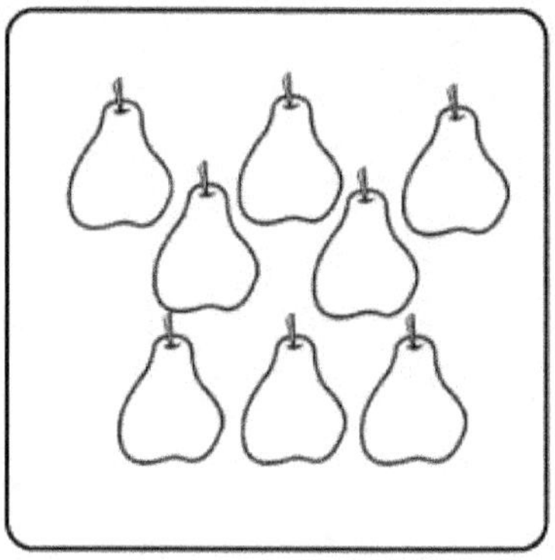

+ 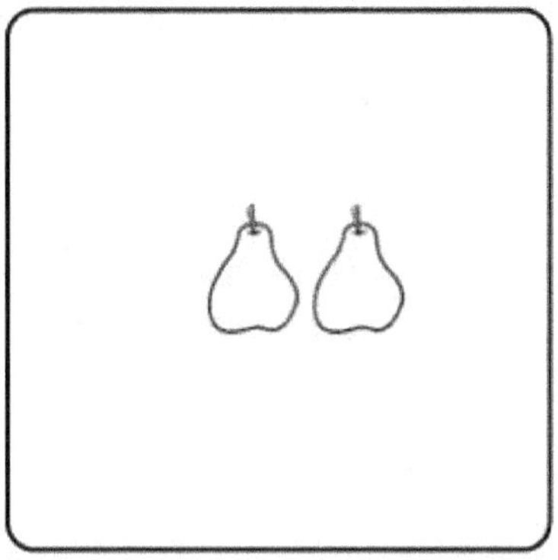 =

+  =

+  =

+  =

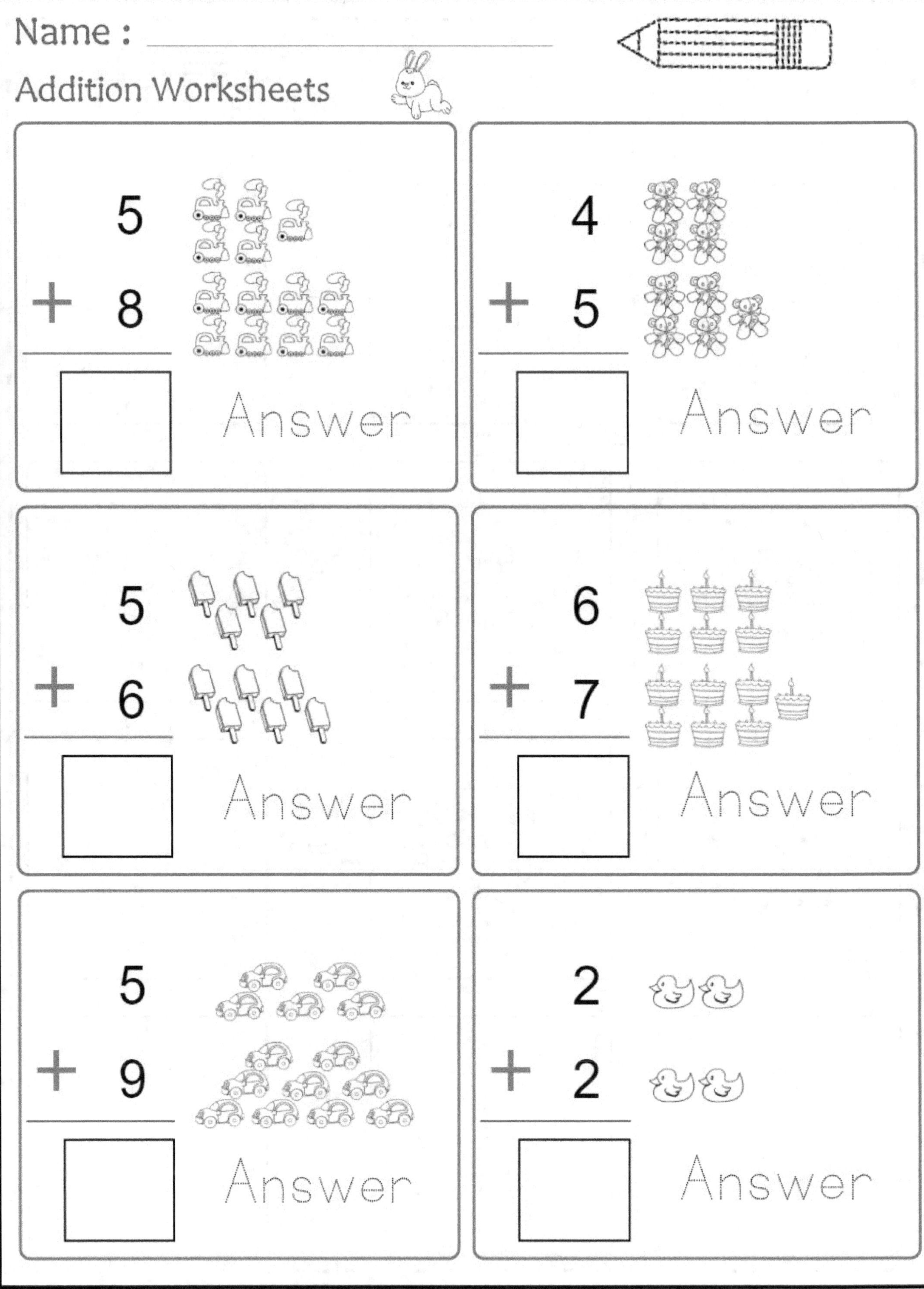
Name :
Addition Worksheets
5
+ 8
Answer
4
+ 5
Answer
5
+ 6
Answer
6
+ 7
Answer
5
+ 9
Answer
2
+ 2
Answer

Name : ______________________

Addition Worksheets

3 + 5 = ☐	20 + 13 = ☐	2 + 8 = ☐
6 + 2 = ☐	6 + 6 = ☐	13 + 4 = ☐
5 + 13 = ☐	14 + 5 = ☐	16 + 12 = ☐

Name : ______________________

Direction: Add the number of images in each box and write the answer in the last box.

+  =

+  =

+  =

+  =

Name : ____________________

Addition Worksheets

1
+ 9

Answer

6
+ 6

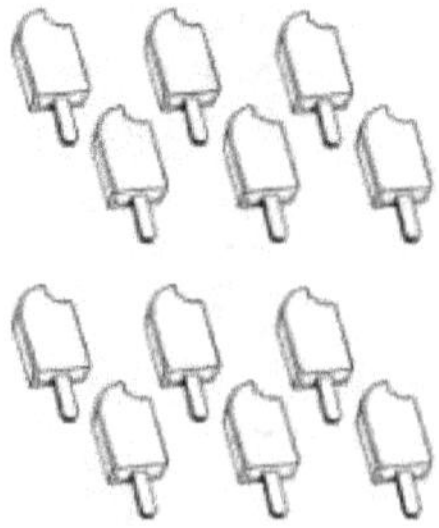

Answer

6
+ 4

Answer

3
+ 2

Answer

1
+ 4

Answer

5
+ 3

Answer

Name : ______________________

Addition Worksheets

9 + 6 = ☐	13 + 8 = ☐	8 + 10 = ☐
14 + 6 = ☐	17 + 1 = ☐	9 + 4 = ☐
20 + 14 = ☐	19 + 6 = ☐	7 + 14 = ☐

Name : ____________________

Direction: Add the number of images in each box and write the answer in the last box.

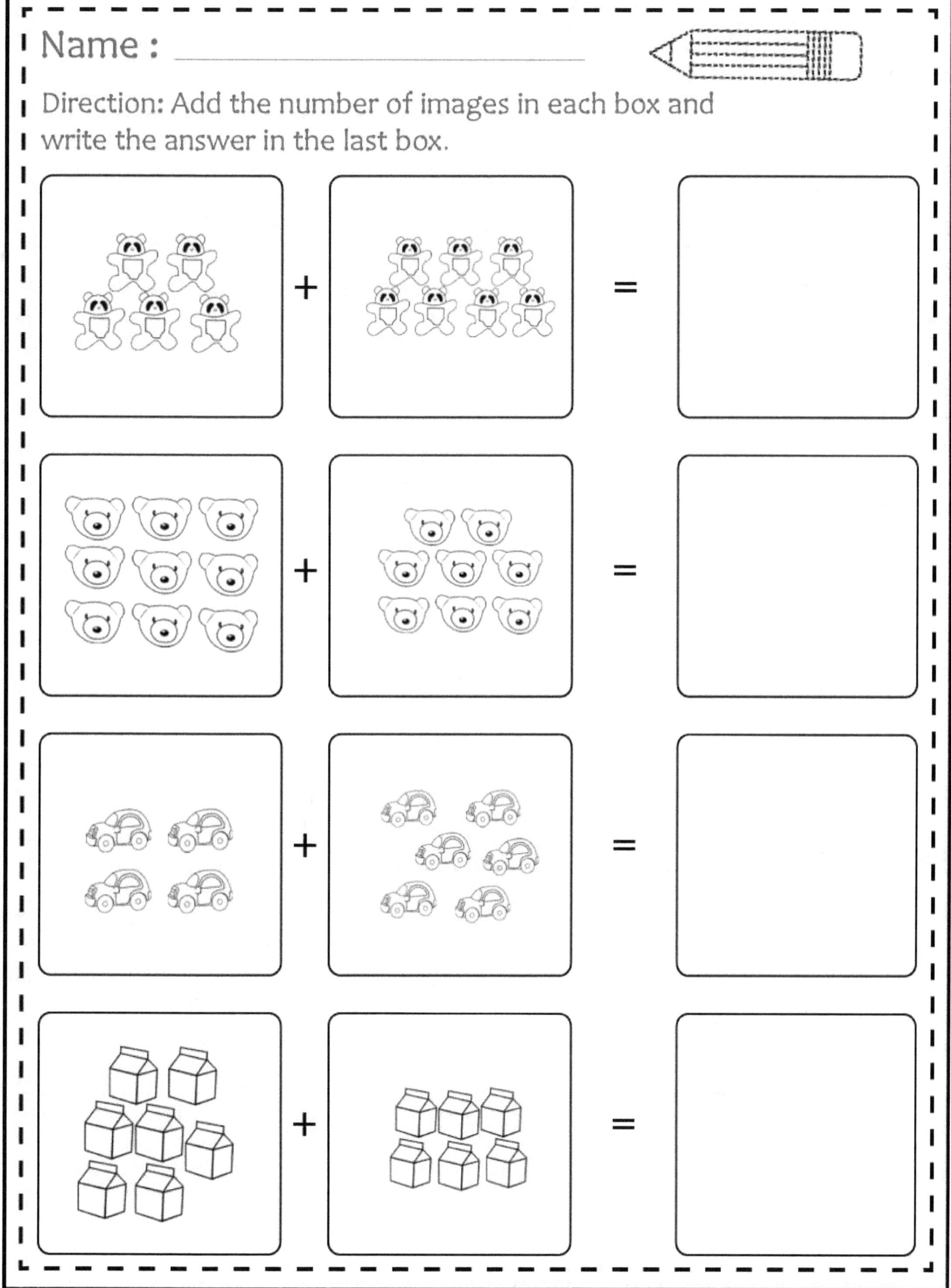

Name : ____________________

Addition Worksheets

5
+ 6

Answer

1
+ 2

Answer

4
+ 6

Answer

2
+ 4

Answer

3
+ 4

Answer

5
+ 4

Answer

Name : ______________________

Addition Worksheets

11 + 16 = ☐	14 + 13 = ☐	14 + 14 = ☐
8 + 18 = ☐	13 + 18 = ☐	4 + 7 = ☐
7 + 11 = ☐	1 + 15 = ☐	13 + 15 = ☐

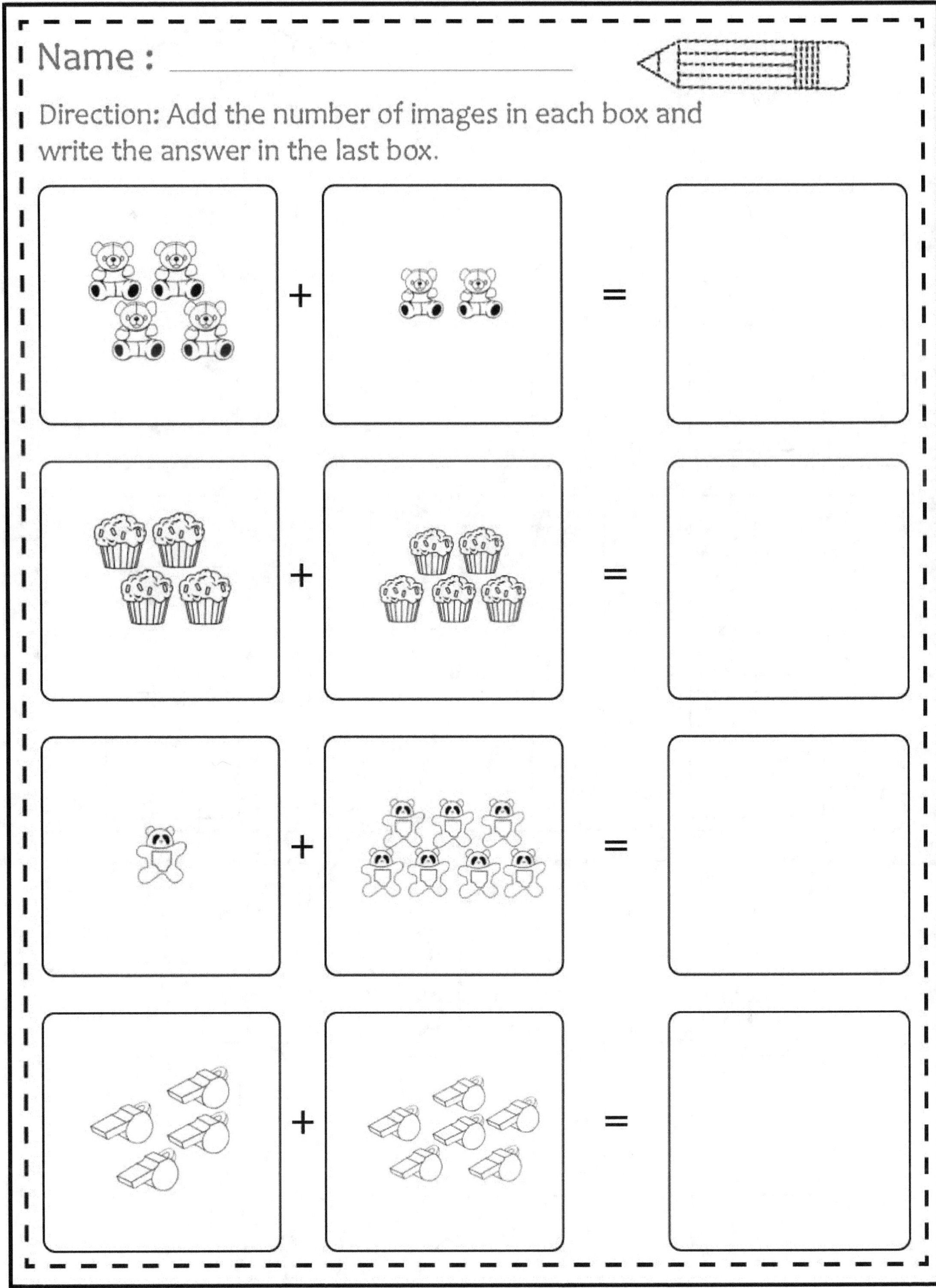

Name :
Direction: Add the number of images in each box and write the answer in the last box.
+
=
+
=
+
=
+
=

Name : ______________________________

Addition Worksheets

$$\begin{array}{r} 5 \\ +\ 7 \\ \hline \end{array}$$

☐ Answer

$$\begin{array}{r} 6 \\ +\ 10 \\ \hline \end{array}$$

☐ Answer

$$\begin{array}{r} 3 \\ +\ 4 \\ \hline \end{array}$$

☐ Answer

$$\begin{array}{r} 5 \\ +\ 9 \\ \hline \end{array}$$

☐ Answer

$$\begin{array}{r} 4 \\ +\ 8 \\ \hline \end{array}$$

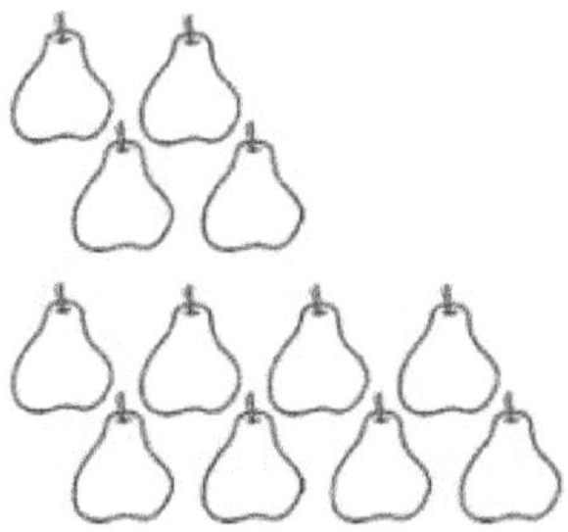

☐ Answer

$$\begin{array}{r} 5 \\ +\ 1 \\ \hline \end{array}$$

☐ Answer

Name : ______________________________

Addition Worksheets

20 + 4 = ☐	9 + 13 = ☐	19 + 9 = ☐
5 + 8 = ☐	9 + 18 = ☐	19 + 7 = ☐
12 + 10 = ☐	1 + 14 = ☐	3 + 13 = ☐

Name : ______________________

Direction: Add the number of images in each box and write the answer in the last box.

+  =

+  =

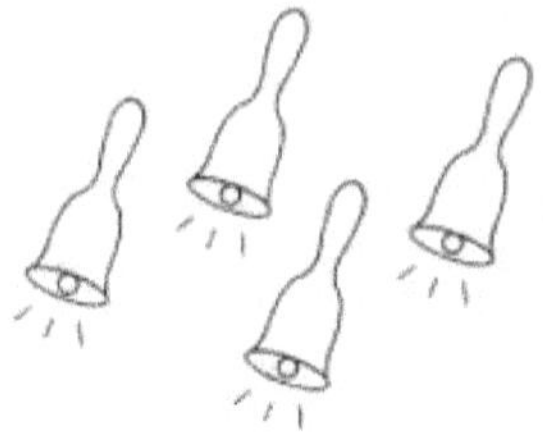

+  =

+  =

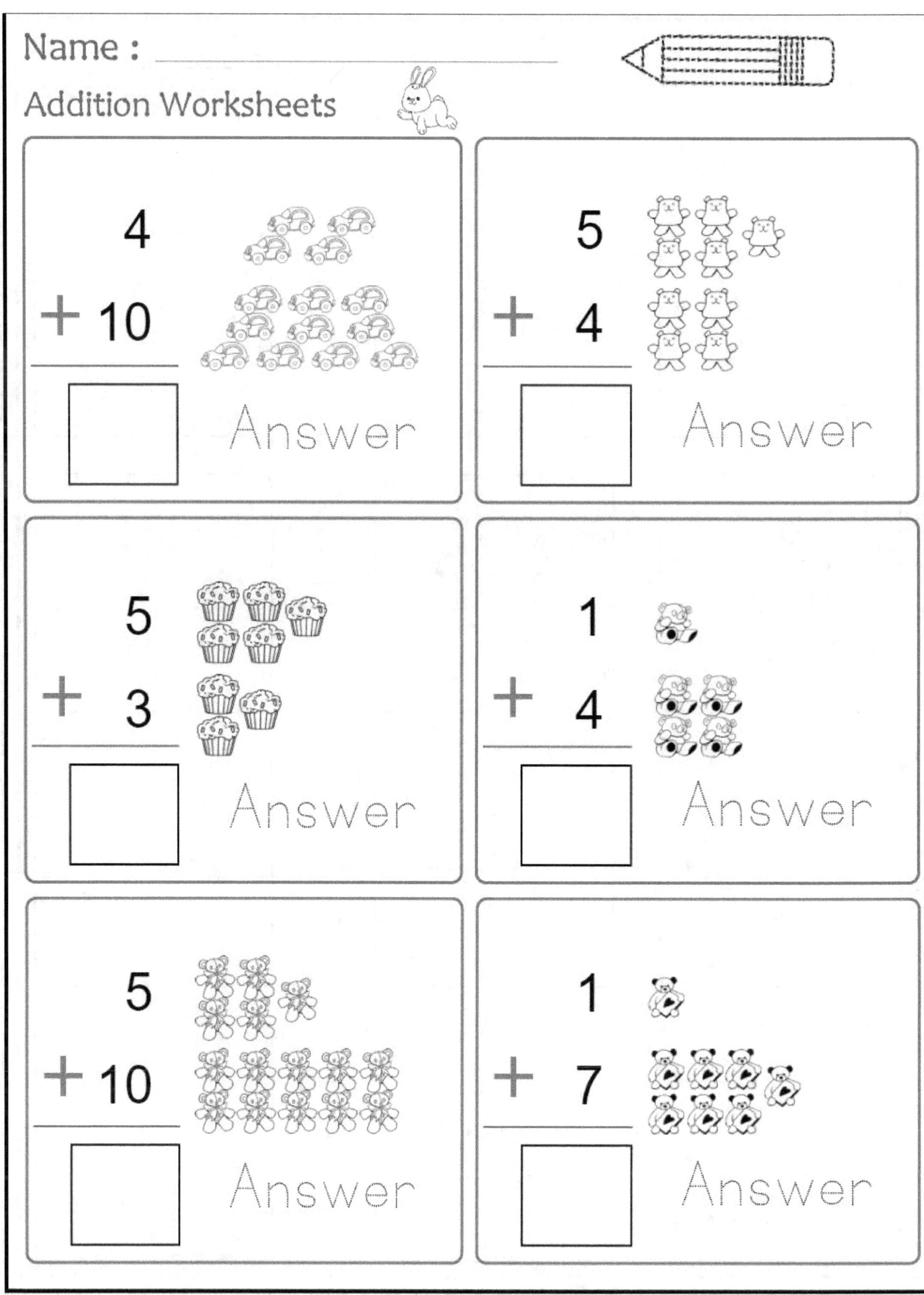

Name :
Addition Worksheets
4
+ 10
Answer
5
+ 4
Answer
5
+ 3
Answer
1
+ 4
Answer
5
+ 10
Answer
1
+ 7
Answer

Name : ______________________

Addition Worksheets

18 + 9 = ☐	7 + 1 = ☐	19 + 4 = ☐
7 + 14 = ☐	4 + 4 = ☐	6 + 16 = ☐
5 + 4 = ☐	19 + 1 = ☐	14 + 10 = ☐

Name : ______________________

Direction: Add the number of images in each box and write the answer in the last box.

+  =

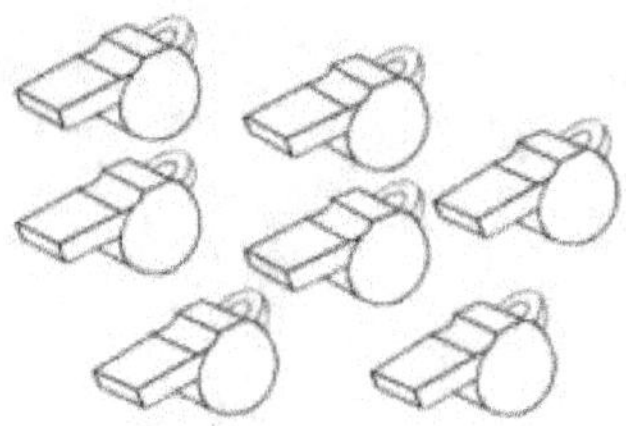

+ 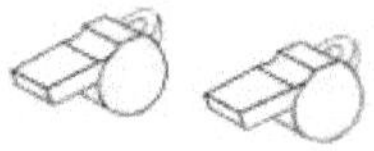 =

+  =

+  =

Name : ______________________

Addition Worksheets

1 + 9 — ☐ Answer	6 + 1 — ☐ Answer
2 + 6 — ☐ Answer	2 + 2 — ☐ Answer
3 + 4 — ☐ Answer	6 + 6 — ☐ Answer

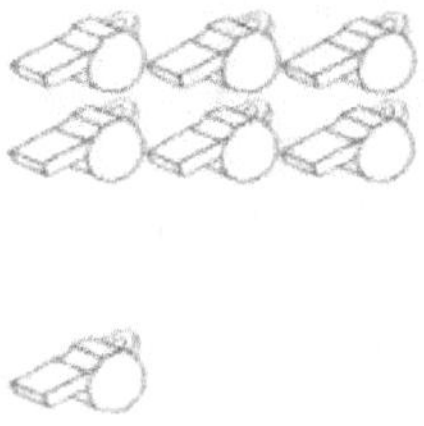

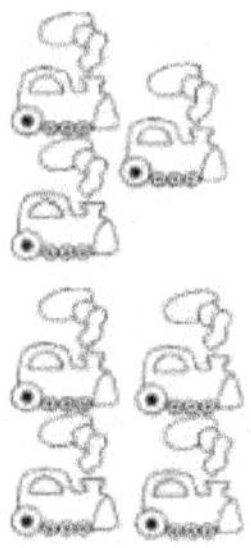

Name : ______________________

Addition Worksheets

11 + 10 = ☐	3 + 7 = ☐	18 + 16 = ☐
9 + 4 = ☐	12 + 16 = ☐	2 + 11 = ☐
2 + 5 = ☐	2 + 17 = ☐	18 + 7 = ☐

Name : ______________________

Direction: Add the number of images in each box and write the answer in the last box.

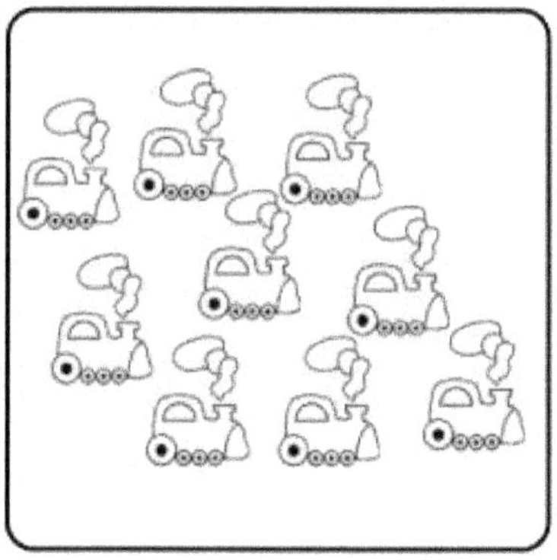

+ 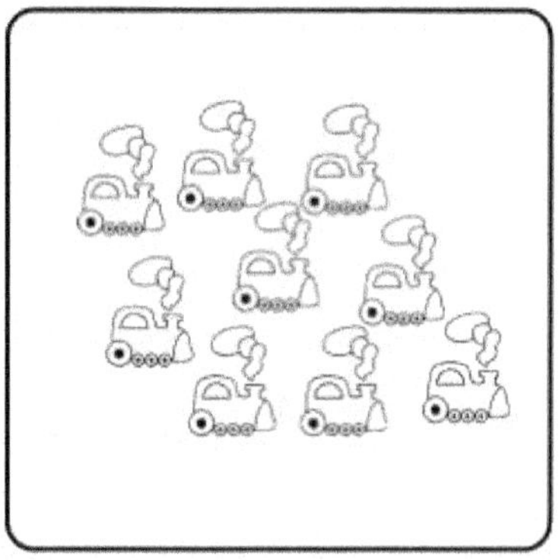 =

+ 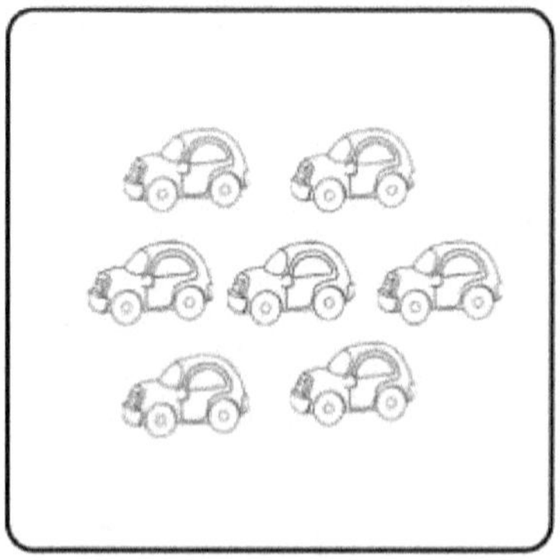 =

+  =

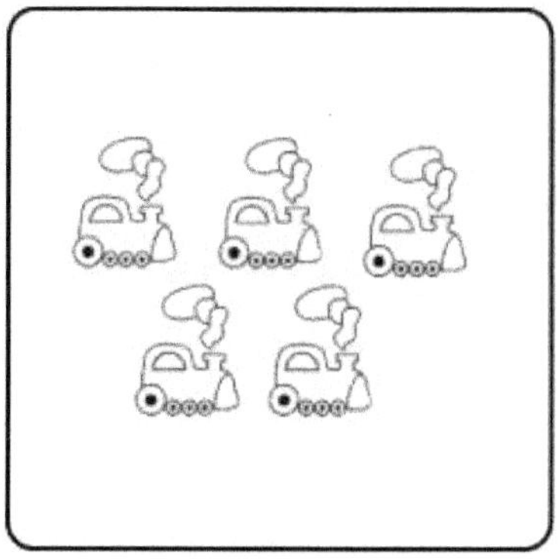

+ 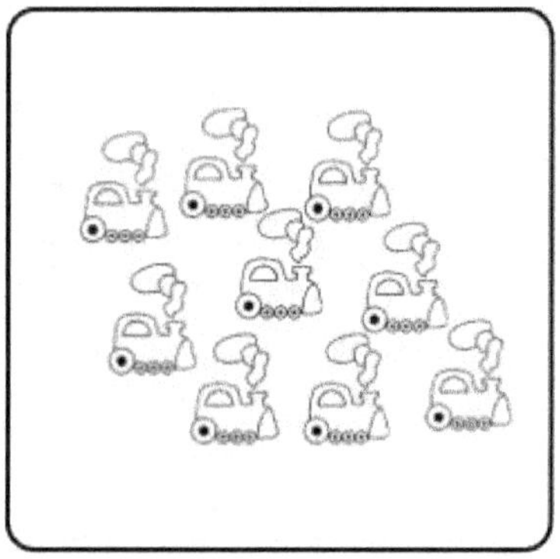 =

Name : ______________________

Addition Worksheets

4
+ 4

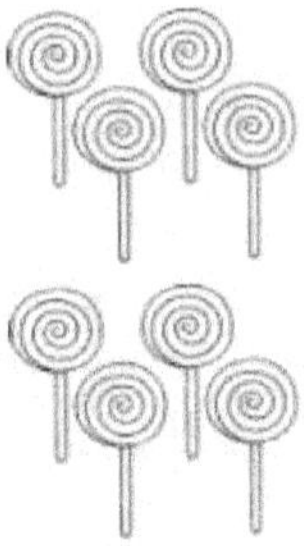

Answer

1
+ 2

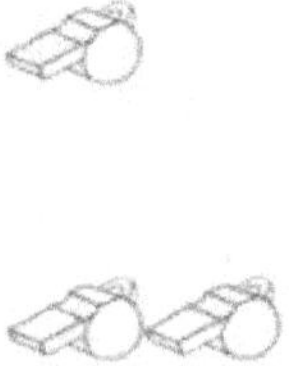

Answer

1
+ 3

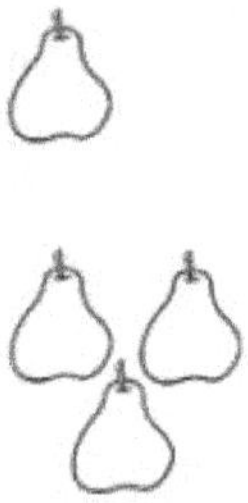

Answer

5
+ 6

Answer

4
+ 1

Answer

4
+ 2

Answer

Name : ______________________

Addition Worksheets

1 + 20	1 + 11	14 + 3
1 + 4	12 + 16	4 + 20
12 + 5	9 + 10	2 + 17

Math Made Easy....

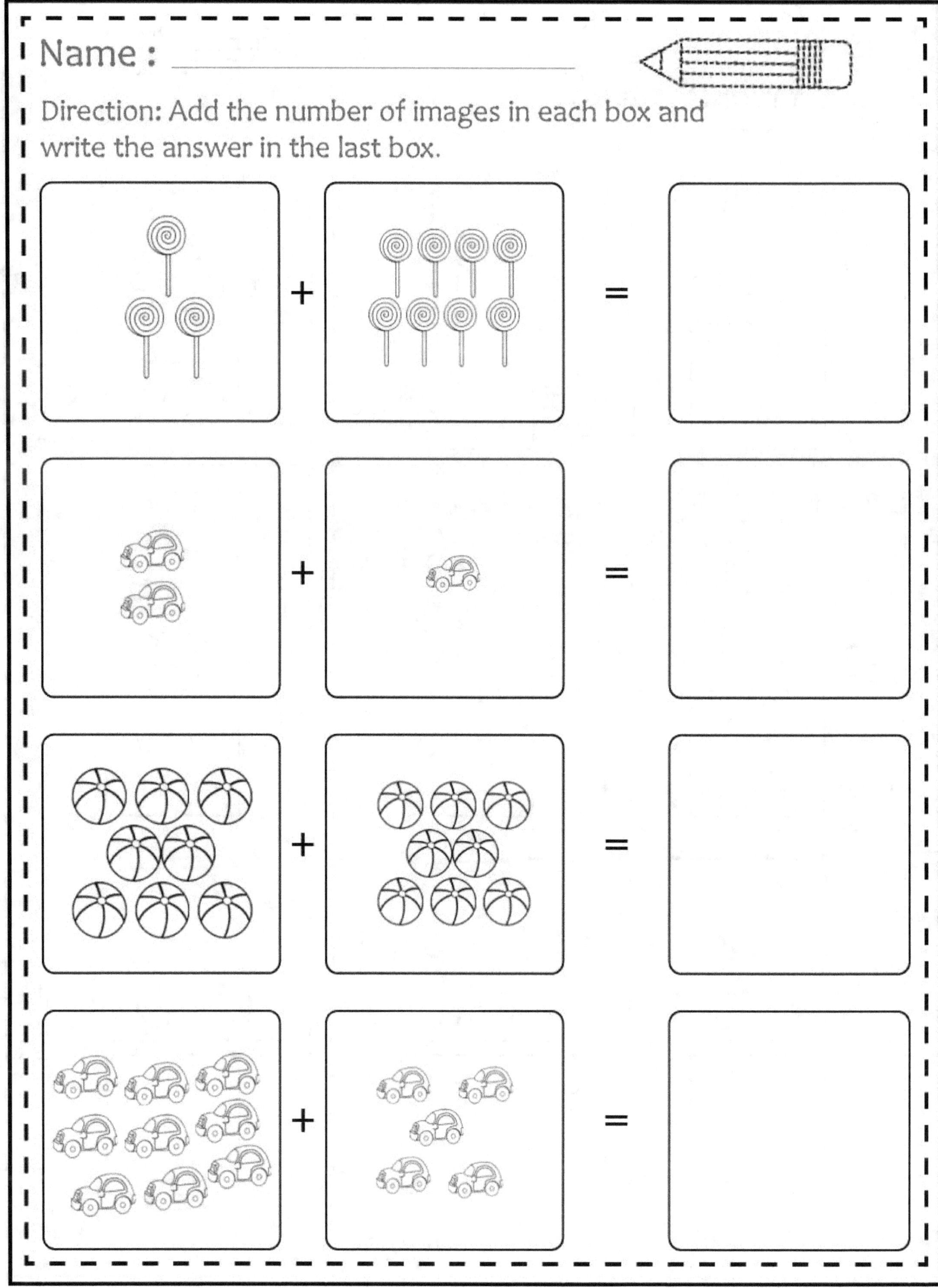

Name :
Direction: Add the number of images in each box and write the answer in the last box.
+
=
+
=
+
=
+
=

Name : ______________________

Addition Worksheets

3 + 6 ___ ☐ Answer	2 + 5 ___ ☐ Answer
5 + 2 ___ ☐ Answer	5 + 4 ___ ☐ Answer
5 + 1 ___ ☐ Answer	5 + 7 ___ ☐ Answer

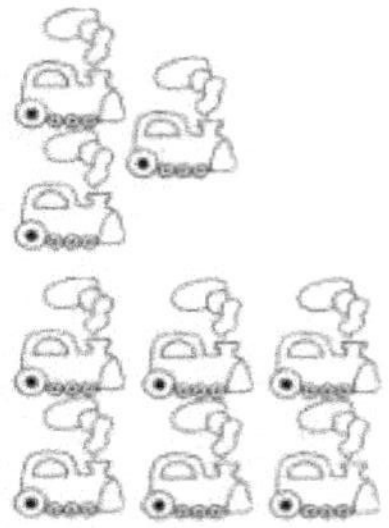

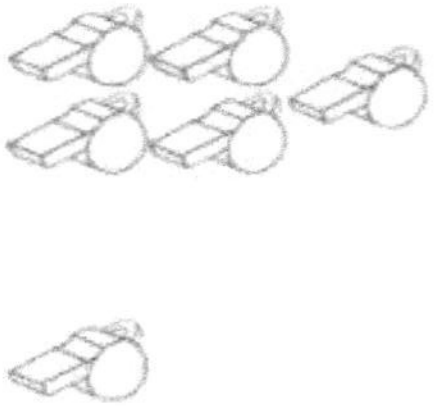

www.ingramcontent.com/pod-product-compliance
Lightning Source LLC
LaVergne TN
LVHW080816170826
845678LV00011B/2025